CORRUPTION

PAITRIK UPADHYAYA

Paitrik Upadhyaya has written a book named corruption his book revolves around curroption and it forms and why they occur .

Contents

Foreword   *vii*

Preface   *ix*

Acknowledgements   *xi*

Prologue   *xiii*

  1. Corruption   1

  2. How To Overcome Corruption   3

Conclusion   7

Foreword

This book is written by Paitrik Upadhyaya currently studying in class 7.

Preface

This book is written to aware people about corruption and causes done through it this book is not intended to harm someone this book is just a diary written by me stating my veiw of point for this particular topic.

Acknowledgements

This is my first book hope you all will like it. Designed this book because of the rapid cases of corruption and what it may rise or it rise this is only my veiw of point for this topic it is not intended to harm. Please enjoy this book like a diary and review it.

Prologue

Corruption is a form of dishonesty or a criminal offense which is undertaken by a person or an organization which is entrusted in a position of authority, in order to acquire illicit benefits or abuse power for one's personal gain. This happens because of greed, desires, political matters, etc. The major factor in this case are: political and economic environment, professional ethics and legislation, as well as purely ethnological factors, such as customs, habits and traditions an this all leads to financial crisis to the people living in a country. People being poor is nothing but this is due to corruption even when you see in collages you have a better rank than other but the other person gets selected whereas you are not selected this is also a form of corruption. In TMC recently the education minister has been raided and ED found 50 cr from his houses and let me clarify that the money that is collected is not of the minister it is our parents who gave him bribe to getjobs in school my friends this form of money is also known as corruption it is known as black money.

ONE

CORRUPTION

Corruption is a form of dishonesty or a criminal offense which is undertaken by a person or an organization which is entrusted in a position of authority, in order to acquire illicit benefits or abuse power for one's personal gain. This happens because of greed, desires, political matters, etc. The major factor in this case are: political and economic environment, professional ethics and legislation, as well as purely ethnological factors, such as customs, habits and traditions an this all leads to financial crisis to the people living in a country. People being poor is nothing but this is due to corruption even when you see in collages you have a better rank than other but the other person gets selected whereas you are not selected this is also a form of corruption. In TMC recently the education minister has been raided and ED found 50 cr from his houses and let me clarify that the money that is collected is not of the minister it is ours one of us a parent gave him bribe to get job in the school my friends this form of money is also known as corruption it is known as black money. In collages many students are their by giving money to the admistration of the collage and sometimes by bribing some successful and creative mind people are not selected and they feel so drippresed that they comit suicide and gave of his life. Albert Einstien was asked to leave the school when he was 15 years old he also felt depressed but he didn't commuted suicide like us rather that he eouncraged himself and created theories on time, gravity, etc if he had commited suicide like us then we won't be able to have knowledge on time, gravity and we can't even imagine ourselves without these so, the main *I would like to tell you that we should never be drippresed and we should never giveup on anything. Some children might don't want to go to school but then if you don't go to school then how would you be able learn maths, English as these days these all revolvolves*

around us and coming back to the point I would like to say that corruption is everywhere and absorb it would be foolishness but to ovbecome with it would be bravery if you don't get admission in university or collage that you want to be in don't get demoralized, depressed, etc there are many universities and collage also in which you should try but don't be like that I think maths is tough for me and opt for commerce without maths in eleventh then you are wrong we should choose the way that is tough as by overcomming it you would realize that nothing is tough in the life it is just that you create a mindsite that it is tough. Corruption is not done for any gain to the subjects it is always done for personal gain.

TWO

HOW TO OVERCOME CORRUPTION

According to analysis, around ninety-two per cent of people have paid government official to get their work done fast or do something out of the law be it a private sector or public sector, India's Corruption is present in every system.Among the top five most corrupted countries of Asia, India tops the list with a seventy per cent bribery rate.According to the World Bank, the grain kept for poor people does not reach them entirely. Only forty per cent reaches them.There are various MLS and MPs who have arrest warrants and tags of Corruption against them. However, even with the guarantees, they can stand for election in India.If you are planning to fight Corruption at the entry level, the best way to do so is through the Right to Information Act of the Indian Constitution.Government offers various schemes for the poor and the mediocre families to enjoy multiple benefits. However, only a small portion of these reaches the people.It will take e huge number of people from different sectors to remove Corruption from India. It is impossible to be conducted by a single person of a particular state.Corruption causes inequalities in society and may also lead to revolt. Denmark is the least corrupt county in the world as per the corruption index table. Somalia is the most corrupt country in the world, followed by Sudan and Syria.Transparency International ranks India at 81st in the global corruption perception table 2017.Corruption has grown to such a level that it has also given rise to many criminal activities.

RTI activists have gone through many attacks for exposing corruption and promoting transparency in the functioning of government offices. In 2106, the Indian government did "Demonetization" to destroy black money. Black money is the main product of corruption which is earned illegally through unfair means. Government corruption occurs when a ruling party takes on a more invasive and pervasive role. Forms of government corruption include nepotism, bribery, lobbying, embezzlement, and cronyism. For instance, a government official may use their power and influence to grant family members high-ranking positions. In other cases, officials may try to sway election results or harm opponents to hold onto power.Corruption is an evil that spreads its poison in the root of nation.A corrupt person takes bribe from people, and in return do illegal work. Corruption increase day by day because there is a secure connection between officials, politicians and criminals who are making this country weaker and weaker.

Conclusion

We should not be demoralized and we should put more efforts to acheive and not everyboody is corrupted so, it is always advisible that we should bring the incedents of corruption to light so, that people are aware and we should spread more awaerness. The best way to remove corruption is to be more vocal about corruption and people should be educated and education and correct guidence is the best tool to eliminate corruption from the society. Educate the new generation about the ill impacts of corruption or about any such cases. Through the Corruption Act, 1988 and the Indian Penal Code, 1860 law made by the goverment states that the social impact of corruption is made visible; this generates awareness in society about the consequences of this scourge and creates new alliances in the fight against corruption. Hence, this states that the goverment which is not corrupted in many ways also, helps ut to end this evil poison named as corruption from the roots of nations. Corruption also make people poor by incresing cost and reducing access to services, including health, education and justice. Nepotism is also a very big example of corruption. Scam is also an example of corruption like, the 1992 scam was a systematic fraud committed by Harshad Mehta in the Indian stock market which led to the complete collapse of security systems. He committed a scam of over 1 billion from the banking system to buy stocks on the Bombay Stock Exchange.Corruption is mainly done by public officials. Public Officials doing corruption states that-: They are dishonest, baised or partial, breach of public interest and involves a misues of information or materials. It's not only goverment employees that can be corrupt. If any private company works for the good of the country then it is stated that they are also public officials. If the corruption is done in massive lead and that is caught by the goverment then it states that its a crime, disciplinary offence, ground of dismisaal,etc. Black money is that currency on which tax is not paid. In a country 1 to 2% people only pay the tax rest 99% people don't pay the tax. People whod don't pay the tax thinks that their money is not goint to safe hands (in this statement safe hands is stated to goverment) as they think that there money is being given to corrupt politicians and to build this trust I think goverment should post all the transactions that they are making from the tax so, that people can get that were their money is going or is it getting utilized correctly or not. Demonatization done by the goverment was not successful as India got 2 to

7% loss in currency and even more than 4,00,000 jobs were affected so, it is very important to remove corruption from that roots of the nation.